DISCOVER 🐾 DOGS WITH THE AMERICAN CANINE ASSOCIATION

AMERICAN CANINE ASSOCIATION, INC.
ACA
America's Largest Veterinary Health Tracking Canine Registry
OFFICIAL SEAL ®

♥ ♥ ♥ ♥ ♥ ♥ ♥ I LIKE ♥ ♥ ♥ ♥ ♥ ♥ ♥
LABRADOR RETRIEVERS!

Linda Bozzo

It is the Mission of the American Canine Association (ACA) to provide registered dog owners with the educational support needed for raising, training, showing, and breeding the healthiest pets expected by responsible pet owners throughout the world. Through our activities and services, we encourage and support the dog world in order to promote best-known husbandry standards as well as to ensure that the voice and needs of our customers are quickly and properly addressed.

Our continued support, commitment, and direction are guided by our customers, including veterinary, legal, and legislative advisors. ACA aims to provide the most efficient, cooperative, and courteous service to our customers, and strives to set the standard for education and problem solving for all who depend on our services.

For more information, please visit www.acacanines.com, e-mail customerservice@acadogs.com, phone 1-800-651-8332, or write to the American Canine Association at PO Box 121107, Clermont, FL 34712.

Enslow Elementary, an imprint of Enslow Publishers, Inc.

Enslow Elementary® is a registered trademark of Enslow Publishers, Inc.

Library of Congress Cataloging-in-Publication Data

Bozzo, Linda.

I like labrador retrievers! / Linda Bozzo.

    p. cm. — (Discover dogs with the american canine association)

Includes bibliographical references and index.

Summary: "Early readers will learn how to care for a Labrador retriever, including breed-specific traits and needs"—Provided by publisher.

ISBN 978-0-7660-3848-6

1. Labrador retriever—Juvenile literature. I. Title.

SF429.L3B69 2012

636.752'7—dc22

                                        2011010475

Future editions:

Paperback ISBN 978-1-4644-0120-6

ePUB ISBN 978-1-4645-1027-4

PDF ISBN 978-1-4646-1027-1

Printed in China

012012 Leo Paper Group, Heshan City, Guangdong, China

10 9 8 7 6 5 4 3 2 1

To Our Readers: We have done our best to make sure all Internet Addresses in this book were active and appropriate when we went to press. However, the author and the publisher have no control over and assume no liability for the material available on those Internet sites or on other Web sites they may link to. Any comments or suggestions can be sent by e-mail to comments@enslow.com or to the address on the back cover.

Every effort has been made to locate all copyright holders of material used in this book. If any errors or omissions have occurred, corrections will be made in future editions of this book.

Photo Credits: Angelika Fischer/Photos.com, p. 13 (hamburger); Annette Shaff/Photos.com, p. 13 (collar); Beatrice Preve/Photos.com, p. 19; Garry Hampton/Photos.com, p. 3 (right); Gina Smith/Photos.com, p. 8; © iStockphoto.com/Shawn Gearhart, p. 21; jclegg/Photos.com, p. 13 (leash and rope); Jupiterimages/Photos.com, p. 5; Shutterstock.com, pp. 1, 3 (left), 4, 6, 9, 10, 11, 13 (Lab, bed, brush, bowls), 16, 17, 18, 23; Viorel Sima/Photos.com, p. 22; © Young-Wolff Photography/Alamy, p. 14.

Cover Photo: Pumba1/Photos.com (black Labrador retriever puppy).

Enslow Elementary

an imprint of

Enslow Publishers, Inc.

40 Industrial Road

Box 398

Berkeley Heights, NJ 07922

USA

http://www.enslow.com

CONTENTS

IS A LABRADOR RETRIEVER RIGHT FOR YOU?

Labrador retrievers, or Labs, are great pets for families with children. They are gentle and smart. They are easy to train. They come in three colors: yellow, black, and brown.

Labrador retrievers are popular work dogs and hunting dogs. This Lab is a guide dog. He helps blind people get around.

Labrador retrievers love to cuddle!

Puppies are full of energy. Can your family keep up?

A DOG OR PUPPY?

Labrador retriever puppies need lots of playtime and training. They need more attention than older dogs. Older dogs may already be trained and might enjoy lying by your side. Would a puppy or older dog be better for your family?

Labs grow to be medium to large dogs. Males are bigger than females.

LOVING YOUR LABRADOR RETRIEVER

Labrador retrievers love playing and going to places like the beach or camping. Do fun things with him to show him your love.

Labrador retrievers love being outdoors.

You can play a Frisbee® game with your Labrador retriever!

EXERCISE

Labrador retrievers need lots of exercise. They enjoy long walks on a leash and playing **fetch**. They also love a good swim.

FEEDING YOUR LABRADOR RETRIEVER

Labrador retrievers can be fed wet or dry dog food. Ask a **veterinarian (vet)**, a doctor for animals, which food to feed your dog and how much to feed her. Give her fresh, clean water every day.

Remember to keep your dog's food and water dishes clean. Dirty dishes can make her sick.

Do not feed your dog people food. It can make her sick.

Your new dog will need:

a collar with a tag

a bed

a brush

food and water dishes

a leash

toys

GROOMING

Labrador retrievers can have skin problems, so they should only be bathed about every six to eight weeks. Use a gentle soap made just for dogs.

Brush your Lab often. Labs **shed** a lot. This means their hair falls out. You also need to clip your dog's nails. A vet or **groomer** can show you how.

WHAT YOU SHOULD KNOW

If these dogs get bored, they may chew and dig. They need to be checked carefully for health problems. If they are healthy, they can make great family pets.

Get your dog toys to keep him busy.

Labrador retrievers like to dig when they are bored.

You will need to take your new dog to the vet for a checkup. He will need shots, called vaccinations, and yearly checkups to keep him healthy. If you think your dog may be sick or hurt, call your vet.

A GOOD FRIEND

Labrador retrievers live up to ten to twelve years. If you feed, play with, and take care of your dog, he will be a good friend to you for a long time.

FUN FACT: Labrador retrievers have a double coat. The first layer is soft and close to the skin. The second layer is longer and rougher. Double coats keep them warm and dry while swimming in cold waters or playing in the snow.

NOTE TO PARENTS

It is important to consider having your dog spayed or neutered when the dog is young. Spaying and neutering are operations that prevent unwanted puppies and can help improve the overall health of your dog.

It is also a good idea to microchip your dog, in case he or she gets lost. A vet will implant a microchip under the skin that contains your contact information, which can then be scanned at a vet's office or animal shelter.

Some towns require licenses for dogs, so be sure to check with your town clerk.

For more information, speak with a vet.

There are many dogs, young and old, waiting to be adopted from animal shelters and rescue groups.

fetch—To go after a toy and bring it back.

groomer—A person who bathes and brushes dogs.

shed—When dog hair falls out so new hair can grow.

vaccinations—Shots that dogs need to stay healthy.

veterinarian (vet)—A doctor for animals.

Books

Landau, Elaine. *Labrador Retrievers Are the Best!* Minneapolis, Minn.: Lerner Publications, 2010.

Mathea, Heidi. *Labrador Retrievers.* Edina, Minn.: ABDO Pub., 2011.

Internet Addresses

American Canine Association Inc., Kids Corner
<http://acakids.com/>

Janet Wall's How to Love Your Dog: The Labrador Retriever
<http://loveyourdog.com/labs.html>

INDEX